TO JASMINE.

LOVE UNCLE ADAM

&

AUNTIE ERIN

IT'S JUST A PLANT

a children's story about marijuana

written & illustrated by Ricardo Cortés

with an afterward by Marsha Rosenbaum, Ph.D.

Jackie loved to go to sleep at night.

Before she got tucked in, her mother would help her walk on her hands… all the way to bed.

One night Jackie woke up past her bedtime.

She smelled something funny in the air,
so she walked down the hall
to her parents' bedroom.

"What's that, Mommy?" asked Jackie. "Are you and Daddy smoking a cigarette?"

"No, baby," said her mother. "This is a *joint*. It's made of marijuana."

"Mar-a-whahh?" asked Jackie, sleepily.

"Marijuana," smiled her dad, "is a plant."

"What kind of plant?"

"Well..." said her mom, "how about we go on a bicycle ride tomorrow, and I will tell you all about it. Okay?"

"Okay," said Jackie.

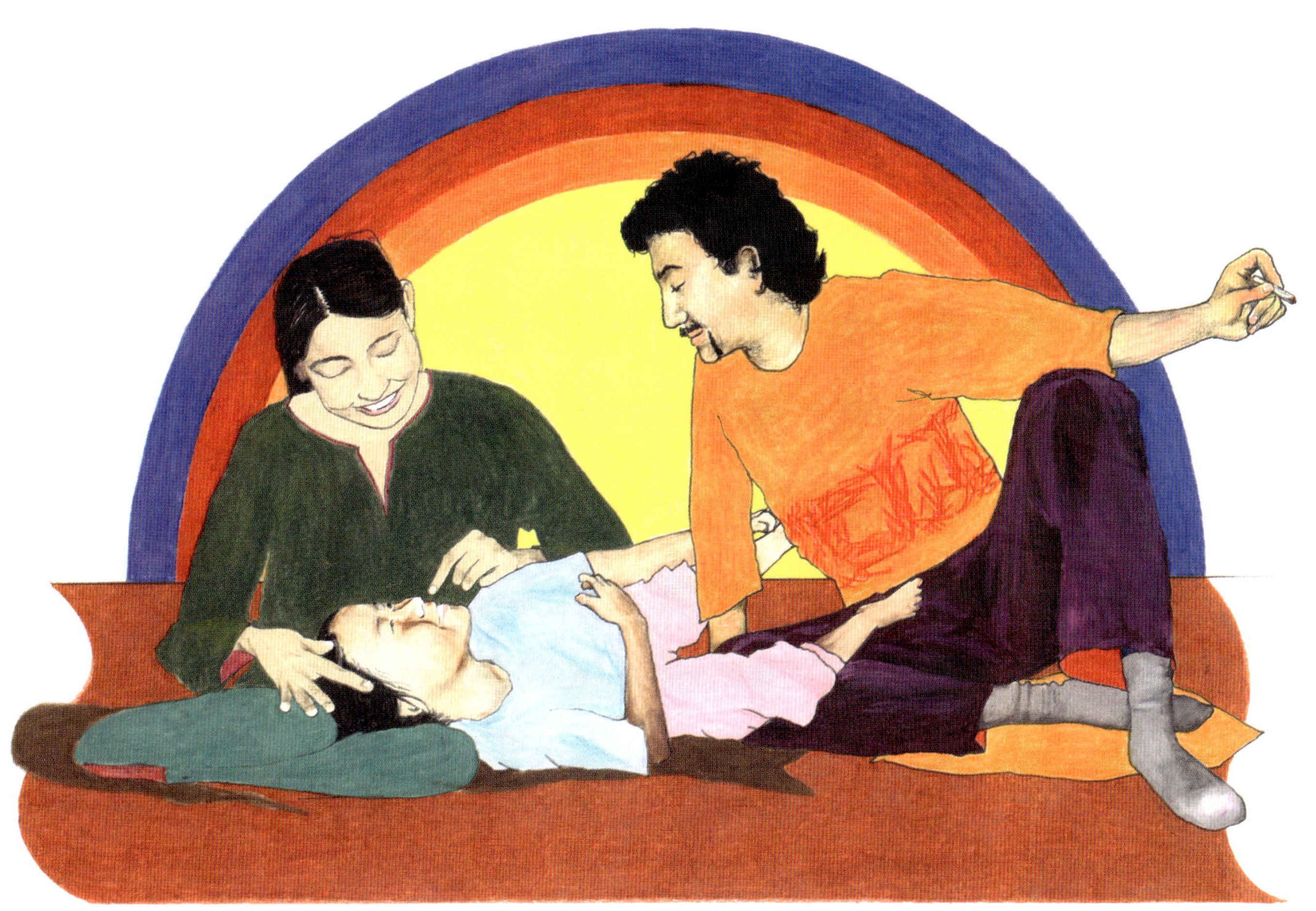

The next day Jackie woke up early to get ready for her adventure, when she remembered...

It was Halloween!

After a big breakfast, Jackie and her mother put on costumes. Then the two of them hopped onto bikes and began their journey.

6
Km

Their first trip was to the farm where Jackie's mother got her vegetables.

"Farmer Bob?" she called out.

"Hi there," said the farmer, coming out from behind a corn patch. "Nice costumes!"

"I came to teach my daughter about marijuana," said Jackie's mom.

"You've come to the right place," answered Bob. "I've got some growing right now. Let's go look."

Farmer Bob walked Jackie and her mom through his garden, stopping to point out the different plants.

He grew so many! There were avocados, cacti, figs, and even mint growing by a strawberry patch. Mmm!

Finally he reached a pot with a sweet, skunky smell.

"This," said Bob, "is a marijuana plant."

“This plant lives all around the world,” he said.

“It can grow very tall with long green leaves. Or, it can be short, fuzzy and purple! Marijuana has been cultivated for thousands of years—just like fruits, beans, and grains.”

“Is marijuana a fruit?” asked Jackie.

“You could say it is,” said Bob. “It grows flowers to make its seeds. I pick the seeds to make food and oil. I clip the flowers and dry them.”

“What do you do with the flowers?” asked Jackie.

“My friends eat them,” said Bob, “and smoke ‘em.”

“They smoke flowers?!”

“Yep. It makes some people feel happy.
Other people say it’s ‘dreamy.’”

“Why do you use it, Farmer Bob?” asked Jackie.

“I don’t,” he said. “It just puts me to sleep!”

"Wow," said Jackie, after they left.
"I'm going to plant some marijuana at home!"

"We'll talk about that later," said her mom.
"Now we're going to see my doctor, Dr. Eden.
I think she will have some more information for us."

Dr. Eden had a very colorful office.

The receptionist said Jackie and her mother could come right in.

“Marijuana,” said Dr. Eden, “is used for many reasons. Like many plants, it can be medicinal. It can heal pain, it helps some people relax, and it calms the stomach to help sick people eat better.”

“Will it help me if I use it?” asked Jackie.

“Marijuana is for people who can use it responsibly. It gives some people joy, but like everything, it can be used too much. I don’t recommend it for everyone. It’s a strong medicine – not good for you right now.”

E
MPM
TZKD
LREJVSH
GAZDKBCI

Jackie and her mother left Dr. Eden's office, with her words and beautiful pictures floating through their heads.

"Marijuana is for grown-ups," said Jackie's mom. "Some things are for adults and not for children, like driving a car or drinking a coffee."

Suddenly, Jackie stopped to sniff the air.

"I know that smell!" she said....

SUBWAY
IMAGINE
T

"YOU'RE SMOKING MARIJUANA!"
yelled out Jackie.

Four men on the corner, taken by surprise, started laughing when they saw Jackie and her mother.

"Excuse me, Miss," said one man,
"I call this *la la*."

"And I," said another, "call it *ganja*."

"I call it *cannabis sativa*," said the third.

"Oh?" said the fourth. "I call it... herb, reefer, muggles, sinsemilla, cheeba cheeba, and weee–"

Before he could even finish, two police officers drove up and told the men to turn around and put their hands up against the wall!

Jackie looked at an officer and asked him, "Mister, why are you arresting these people?"

"Young lady," answered the policeman, "These men were smoking what *I* call grass, and that is against the law."

"Grass isn't against the law!" said Jackie.

"Hmm," he said. "Let me tell you..."

"People were once allowed to smoke marijuana," began the police officer.

"My grandfather grew it and made cloth from the plant's stalk. Others made rope or paper from it. My grandmother once ran a café where she sold tea, toast, and cakes made of homegrown grass."

BAKERY
OTTO
LAUNDRY
MARIJUANA
COFFEE
TEA SHOP
THE PRESS
GOVERNMENT
TELLS FARMERS
TO GROW HEMP

"One day, a government decided to make a law against marijuana," continued the officer.

"The government started a war around the world to stop people from growing it. Marijuana became an *illegal* plant. Doctors tried to protest the new law, but the politicians and lawmakers did not listen."

Jackie couldn't believe it!

"Mommy..." she said, "is that all true?"

"It is true," said Jackie's mother.

"Any government can make a bad law," she said. "Luckily, where we live people can work together to fix unfair laws."

"That's true, too," said the officer. "Many police officers don't agree with the law against marijuana. But our job is to enforce rules, not to change them. If you think a law is a mistake, you can work to change it."

SCHOOL NOT WAR
BIKES NOT BOMBS
POOLS NOT JAILS
RACISM
DON'T TREAD ON MY GARDEN!
I'm a MOM!
REEDOM OF RELIGION
TIME FOR A CHANGE

"In the meantime," said the second officer, "we're going to let these men go, with a warning. But other officers may not be so nice. So move along, please."

"Thank you," said the men, as they walked away.

"Thank you!" said Jackie.

That night, Jackie's family ate a dinner of squash, tomato salad, bread, and macaroni.

For a treat, Jackie's mom added Farmer Bob's strawberries to their dessert.

"When I grow up," announced Jackie, "I am going to work to make all the laws fair."

After their meal, Jackie's father flew her like an airplane to bed.

"There are many ways to help make change," said her dad. "Maybe you will be a lawyer, or a scientist."

"Or a pilot!" said Jackie.

"Or a dancer," she dreamed.

"Or a newspaper writer...
or a judge... or a gardener...
or a..."

The End

An Epilogue
by Marsha Rosenbaum, Ph.D.

Nearly 80 million Americans admit that they have tried an illegal drug. Many of these former or current users are parents, and the vast majority is in a quandary about what to say to their children about the most widely used illegal drug in the world, marijuana. Whether or not they still use it, parents are eager to learn "the facts" about marijuana. They want to know how to open a discussion with their kids, and most of all, how to keep their children out of harm's way.

When seeking information, parents find plenty of "drug education" publications, websites and advertisements. Most are written by and distributed through local, state and federal agencies. By definition, these publications, which carry the seal of approval of the government, stress the inherent dangerousness of all illegal drugs, including (and today, especially) marijuana, and uniformly recommend a staunch abstinence-only approach. To do otherwise, it is argued, is to condone, even promote experimentation among young people.

As founder of a drug education project for parents, I regularly conduct workshops and answer questions. I've found that concerned parents, barraged with scare tactics initially targeted at their children and now aimed straight at them, find themselves confused, frightened, and even doubting their ability to talk with their own kids. Many parents worry about how much to admit about their own past or present marijuana use. They fear "opening the door" if they say anything at all that is remotely positive about their experiences, and that their children will believe they condone drug use if they offer neutral information and ongoing, supportive conversations.

However, honest conversations and safety-oriented offers of help, if and when needed, do not open the door to marijuana use. In America today, where as a society we regularly imbibe and medicate with a variety of legal and illegal substances, the door to drug use is already wide open. To deny the reality of the role of drug use in our culture, to cling to worn out doomsday messages, and deny our kids help and support when they need it, is to expose them to risk and danger far beyond marijuana use.

It's Just a Plant provides parents of young children with a realistic tool that enables them, through reading together, to open early discussions about marijuana. The book succeeds in helping parents send two important messages: Marijuana has a long history and various uses, and whereas adults can use it responsibly, *it is not to be used by children.*

What a refreshing alternative to the outdated options that dominate today's programs and messages!

***Marsha Rosenbaum**, **Ph.D**, is founder of the **Safety First Project** for drug education and director emerita of the San Francisco office of the **Drug Policy Alliance**, the nation's leading organization working to end the war on drugs. From 1977 to 1995, she was the principal investigator on several National Institute on Drug Abuse-funded studies on drug use. Dr. Rosenbaum is the author of numerous books and scholarly articles about drug use, addiction, treatment and drug policy. She regularly speaks to PTAs, other parent groups, schools, drug treatment and prevention professionals and the media about teenagers and drugs, and drug policy issues. She is also a parent.*

For more information, please visit: ***www.drugpolicy.org***

Third Edition 2011

Library of Congress Control Number: 2011911592
ISBN-13: 978-0-9760117-6-7
Manufactured in China through Asia Pacific Offset, September 2011
This product conforms to CPSIA 2008
10 9 8 7 6 5 4 3 2 1

This book was fun to make. Thank you!

About the author...

Ricardo Cortés has written and illustrated many books, including *Go the Fuck to Sleep, I Don't Want to Blow You Up!,* and *Coffee, Coca & Cola.*

Visit him at: **RMCORTES.COM**

Extra credits: Jackie's father wears a shirt by Tillamook Cheddar. Farmer Bob's garden has a sculpture of a fish by V. Court Johnson. The waiting room at Dr. Eden's office has art by Futura, TOO FLY, SMARCUS, and Joshua Humphries. The men on the corner wear tees by Taagen/Rockers, and Shemale Skateboards. The man in the sunglasses is Steve Marcus. The Ocote Soul Sounds mural in front of the bakery is by Pete Neonakis. The woman signing the petition is P.J. Stentz. The painting in Jackie's dining room is by Che Jen. The photo on the red bedroom wall is by Sara Press. Thank you!

Special thanks to Jennifer, Aleyamma, and Melissa, who originally helped me put this book together. Also a big thank you to the Drug Policy Alliance, Law Enforcement Against Prohibition, and especially, my friends and family.

Published by the Magic Propaganda Mill of Brooklyn, New York
www.mpmill.com

www.justaplant.com